North American Indians Today

North American Indians Today

Apache

Cherokee

Cheyenne

Comanche

Creek

Crow

Huron

Iroquois

Navajo

Ojibwa

Osage

Potawatomi

Pueblo

Seminole

Sioux

North American
Indians Today

Seminole

by
Joyce Libal

Mason Crest Publishers
Philadelphia

We would like to thank the Seminole Tribe of Florida and the Seminole Nation of Oklahoma for their help with this book.

Mason Crest Publishers Inc.
370 Reed Road
Broomall, Pennsylvania 19008
(866) MCP-BOOK (toll free)

First printing
1 2 3 4 5 6 7 8 9 10
Library of Congress Cataloging-in-Publication Data on file at the Library of Congress.
ISBN: 1-59084-677-X
1-59084-663-X (series)

Design by Lori Holland.
Composition by Bytheway Publishing Services, Binghamton, New York.
Cover design by Benjamin Stewart.
Printed and bound in the Hashemite Kingdom of Jordan.
Photography by Benjamin Stewart. Picture on p. 6 by Keith Rosco.

Contents

Why is it so important that Indians be brought into the "mainstream" of American life?
I would not know how to interpret this phrase to my people.
The closest I would be able to come would be "a big wide river".
Am I then to tell my people that they are to be thrown into the big, wide river of the United States?

Earl Old Person
Blackfeet Tribal Chairman

Introduction

In the midst of twenty-first-century North America, how do the very first North Americans hold on to their unique cultural identity? At the same time, how do they adjust to the real demands of the modern world? Earl Old Person's quote on the opposite page expresses the difficulty of achieving this balance. Even the common values of the rest of North America—like fitting into the "mainstream"—may seem strange or undesireable to North American Indians. How can these groups of people thrive and prosper in the twenty-first century without losing their traditions, the ways of thinking and living that have been handed down to them by their ancestors? How can they keep from drowning in North America's "big, wide river"?

Thoughts from the Series Consultant

Each of the books in this series was written with the help of Native scholars and tribal leaders from the particular tribe. Based on oral histories as well as written documents, these books describe the current strategies of each Native nation to develop its economy while maintaining strong ties with its culture. As a result, you may find that these books read far differently from other books about Native Americans.

Over the past centuries, Native groups have faced increasing pressure to conform to the wishes of the governments that took their lands. Often brutally inhumane methods were implemented to change Native social systems. These books describe the ways that Native groups refused to be passive recipients of change, even in the face of these past atrocities. Heroic individuals worked to fit external changes into local conditions. This struggle continues today.

The legacy of the past still haunts the psyche of both Native and non-Native people of North America; hopefully, these books will help correct some misunderstandings. And even with the difficulties encountered by past and current Native leaders, Native nations continue to thrive. As this series illustrates, Native populations continue to increase—and they have clearly persevered against incredible odds. North American culture's big, wide river may be deep and cold—but Native Americans are good swimmers!

—*Martha McCollough*

Breaking Stereotypes

One way that some North Americans may "drown" Native culture is by using stereotypes to think about North American Indians. When we use stereotypes to think about a group of people, we assume things about them because of their race or cultural group. Instead of taking time to understand individual differences and situations, we lump together everyone in a certain group. In reality, though, every person is different. More than two million Native people live in North America, and they are as *diverse* as any other group. Each one is unique.

Even if we try hard to avoid stereotypes, however, it isn't always easy to know what words to use. Should we call the people who are native to North America Native Americans—or American Indians—or just Indians?

The word "Indian" probably comes from a mistake—when Christopher Columbus arrived in the New World, he thought he had reached India, so he called the people he found there Indians. Some people feel it doesn't make much sense to call Native Americans "Indians." (Suppose Columbus had thought he landed in China instead of India; would we today call Native people "Chinese"?) Other scholars disagree; for example, Russell Means, Native politician and activist, claims that the word "Indian" comes from Columbus saying the native people were *en Dios*—"in God," or naturally spiritual.

Many Canadians use the term "First Nations" to refer to the Native peoples who live there, and people in the United States usually speak of Native Americans. Most Native people we talked to while we were writing these books prefer the simple term "Indian"—or they would rather use the names of their tribes. (We have used the term "North American Indians" for our series to distinguish this group of people from the inhabitants of India.)

Even the definition of what makes a person "Indian" varies. The U.S. government recognizes certain groups as tribal nations (almost 500 in all). Each nation then decides how it will enroll people as members of that tribe. Tribes may require a particular amount of Indian blood, tribal membership of the father or the mother, or other *criteria*. Some enrolled tribal members who are legally "Indian" may not look Native at all; many have blond hair and blue eyes and others have clearly African features. At the same time, there are thousands of Native people whose tribes have not yet been officially recognized by the government.

We have done our best to write books that are as free from stereotypes as possible. But you as the reader also play a part. After reading one of these books, we hope you won't think: "The Cheyenne are all like this" or "Iroquois are all like that." Each person in this world is unique, whatever their culture. Stereotypes shut people's minds—but these books are intended to open your mind. North American Indians today have much wisdom and beauty to offer.

Some people consider American Indians to be a historical topic only, but Indians today are living, contributing members of North American society. The contributions of the various Indian cultures enrich our world—and North America would be a very different place without the Native people who live there. May they never be lost in North America's "big, wide river"!

An alligator swims in the Everglades' dark water.

Chapter 1

Early History

Che-hun-tah-mo!
("Welcome!" in the Miccosukee language.)

Several pairs of alligator eyes glide like quiet *periscopes* above the surface of the still water. Purple irises stand at attention in sedate pools. Turtles sun themselves on protruding logs. Birds provide a riot of sound as the roaring motor quiets. Allow yourself to float back in time in the heart of the Florida *Everglades*. Imagine that you are no longer in an *airboat* at Billy Swamp Safari, one of the successful businesses run by the Seminole Tribe of Florida at their Big Cypress *Reservation*. As the warm breeze that has been passing across your skin is replaced by still, hot air, think back to a time when the ancestors of the economically successful businesspeople who call the five Florida Seminole Reservations home once traveled this water in dugout canoes. Drift back a century, two centuries, and more.

We do not know exactly when people first arrived in this land. When Ponce de León stepped onto the coast of what he called La Florida in 1513, *indigenous* groups had already inhabited the area for centuries. The Europeans brought tragedy to these original inhabitants in many forms; however, the first, and one of the most deadly, was disease. *Tuberculosis*, *smallpox*, and measles were among the horrors that *decimated* native populations. Some who avoided illness fell prey to slavery and were stolen away from friends and family forever.

Among the ancestors of the brave and independent people who would come to be known as the Seminole were the Creek people, who began arriving from Georgia and reinhabiting Florida in the early 1700s. To a much lesser extent, the ancestors of today's Seminole grew to include more nationalities, such as the Scottish men who arrived during the eighteenth century with customs and dress that had some similarity to that of the Creek. The British also gained a presence among the people. The Creeks soon expanded their hunting, gathering, and agricultural lifestyle to include trapping and trade with the Europeans. By the mid-1700s, established Creek (Seminole) settlements were in Florida. The Europeans' insatiable desire for land to grow crops like cotton, and trade that introduced items such as cloth (and later sewing machines) to the Seminole people, strongly influenced the Seminole way of life.

The growing of cotton was also one of the reasons for the forced importation of African people to North America. The Seminole were among the

Chickees were easily constructed homes for the early inhabitants of Florida.

Recreations of dugout canoes like those used by the early Seminole.

first people to demonstrate **tolerance** and **empathy** to African Americans; the Seminole proved by their actions that they believed in the **credo**, "all men are created equal." Both runaway slaves and freedpersons were often welcomed into the Seminole camps or lived in their own communities in close **proximity** to the Seminole. Many of these people became trusted advisors and interpreters. Sometimes they married into the tribe, adding yet another influence on the Seminole culture. Some historians suggest that

Chickee

Still prevalent in yards across Southern Florida today, chickees were the standard form of Seminole housing during the Seminole Wars because they could be constructed quickly from the cypress logs and palm thatch that was readily available. Today, Seminole live in brick, stucco, and wooden houses, and people who have chickees use them for cooking and family gatherings in hot weather. A well-made chickee usually lasts about ten years.

because of their experience living in tropical climates, Africans imparted valuable agricultural knowledge to the Indian people who befriended them. For a time, both Indians and Africans living in Florida joined with Spain in protecting the area from the British, but Spain surrendered the area to Britain in 1763.

The Creeks, who began to settle in Florida during the eighteenth century, lived in buildings made of logs. By necessity, this type of housing would later give way to the more easily constructed *chickee*. In addition to food crops, some people also raised cattle, horses, chickens, and hogs. Others depended on hunting and gathering.

In 1790, George Washington and a Creek chief named Alexander McGillivray signed the Treaty of New York, the first of several illegal treaties signed by individuals claiming to represent the Seminole. In it, McGillivray agreed to relinquish land. However, he had no claim to the land he was giving away. Six years later, the Treaty of Coleraine (another illegal treaty since it was signed by a group of Creek chiefs who had no legal right to represent the Seminole) set boundaries for the relinquished land. The group also agreed to return the African people who were living among the Seminole. The Seminole were understandably angry with both the Creeks and the Americans about these false treaties.

This dissatisfaction grew in the nineteenth century as the goal of *assim-*

ilation of native populations took root and grew among officials of the federal government. The American government wanted to acquire Indian land and to make Indian people and their culture "disappear." President Thomas Jefferson charged Colonel Benjamin Hawkins with this task in relation to the Creeks and Seminole. The British fanned the growing flame of anti-American sentiment among the Seminole and used it to their advantage. Thus began a period of unrest as the British fought Americans, and Creek and Seminole lined up on both sides of the battles.

The first of three time periods that would later be referred to as the Seminole Wars began in 1816, and slavery was one of its causes. Plantation owners in Georgia were angry when runaway slaves found a safe haven among the Seminole in Florida. Worried that an increasing number of slaves would seek freedom there, they began to plan a takeover of the area. Having received word of this plan and that a large assault was *imminent*, a group of Seminole decided to strike first. Another battle soon followed at a former British fort, which had been taken over by Seminole and Africans, on Florida's Apalachicola River. Creek Indians, U.S. Marines, and Navy ships attacked the fort in unison. More than 350 African Americans and Seminole were killed or wounded during the battle; survivors were sent back to slavery in Georgia.

During the First Seminole War, forces under the leadership of Andrew Jackson and a Creek chief named William McIntosh repeatedly attacked the Seminole. The Seminole were often forced to leave their villages and give up their established way of life as they took on a more *nomadic* existence in order to flee from their oppressors.

Although a formal declaration of war was not passed by the U.S. Congress, Andrew Jackson continued to fight for control of Florida. The United States purchased Florida from Spain in 1819 for $5 million, and in 1821, President James Monroe installed Andrew Jackson as its first governor. Andrew Jackson became obsessed with the idea of removing all Indians from the southeastern United States.

Under increasing *duress*, the Seminole signed the Treaty of Moultrie Creek in 1823 in which they relinquished all their lands in Florida. Tensions between Seminole and settlers of European descent intensified during a drought in 1825, when starving Seminole were desperate to obtain food. Chief Tukose Emathla tried to decrease tensions by traveling to Washington to explain the Seminole situation. In describing his feelings for his homeland, one Seminole leader is quoted as having said, "Here our navel strings were first cut and the blood from them sunk into the earth and made the country dear to us."

By 1830, Andrew Jackson was the president of the United States. Under his leadership, Congress passed the Indian Removal Act, a bill calling for the removal of all Indians from the eastern United States. Subjected to ever increasing hostility, pressure, and duress, the Seminole were forced to sign yet another treaty in 1832. According to this Treaty of Paynes Landing, the Seminole were to move from Florida to land in present-day Oklahoma. There they would be placed under the leadership of the Creeks, for whom they had developed an intense *animosity*.

A group of Seminole representatives, including seven chiefs, went on an expedition to inspect this foreign western land in 1832. Under threats and *coercion*, the chiefs signed another treaty accepting and approving the property, but upon returning to Florida, they protested the circumstances under which they were forced to sign the document. Tribe members strongly opposed the treaty and bravely refused to leave their homeland. These events led to the Second Seminole War.

One of the first incidents to mark the beginning of the Second Seminole

A modern chickee makes a good picnic shelter.

War, which was to last until 1842, was the killing of *Indian agent* General Wiley Thompson. General Thompson had cruelly and viciously captured Morning Dew, the wife of Osceola (William Powell), a respected and admired member of the Seminole. Morning Dew had an Indian father, but she was also the child of a runaway slave, and this fact sealed her fate with General Thompson. Although she had not previously been a slave, she was captured by General Thompson and

> The Spanish identified Indians living in Florida by the term "cimmaron." The word has been translated as "unruly or wild ones." Muskogee (Creek) people altered the term to simalóni, which also means "runaway or wild." The British further refined the word to Seminole.

never returned. Naturally, Osceola was enraged by this act of injustice and fought to regain the freedom of his beloved wife. General Thompson's reaction was to have Osceola arrested. This *cavalier* decision cost General Thompson his life when Osceola later avenged his wife's capture.

A second incident took place that same year when two other Seminole leaders (Jumper and Alligator) and a group of Seminole men (of both Indian and African descent) successfully ambushed a group of more than a hundred soldiers on their way to Fort King. This incident is sometimes referred to as the Dade Massacre.

In 1836, Major General Thomas Sidney Jessup was put in charge of the Florida campaign. Already hated by the Seminole because of past dishonorable deeds (including holding of women and children as hostages), Major General Jessup used *deception* to capture the revered Seminole leader Osceola and several others (including Indian leader Wild Cat and the African leader John Horse). Wild Cat, John Horse, and several others were able to make a daring escape, but Osceola was ill and died in prison in 1838, the same year that Jessup was replaced by General Zachary Taylor.

General Taylor fought the escapees, who had joined other Seminole at Lake Okeechobee. Though General Taylor would later claim victory, estimates are that between one and ten Seminole lost their lives in the battle, whereas the United States had 140 dead or wounded soldiers. The United States began the attack with approximately one thousand men, while estimates for Seminole engaged in the battle range from dozens to approximately three hundred. Clearly, the Seminole were fierce and effective warriors. Another powerful leader, Abiaka (Sam Jones), was among the Seminole who were the true victors of the Battle of Okeechobee on Christmas Day in 1837.

In the Everglades, runaway slaves and Seminole found many hiding places from their enemies.

During the Second Seminole War, the Seminole were relentlessly pursued, and therefore, they were constantly on the move. Imagine the sadness and hardship that being constantly uprooted from their homes must have caused to families, especially if they had to care for young children or sick or elderly members. Chickees were constructed and abandoned as necessary for continued mobility. Families often had to leave all material goods behind while fleeing for their lives. The vastly outnumbered but intelligent Seminole engaged in a sort of guerrilla warfare, ambushing soldiers when opportunity presented itself and retreating into the swamps for safety as necessary.

When Seminole were captured, they were scheduled for removal from Florida. Usually this was done without regard for families or relationships. Captured people of African descent were sometimes turned over to white people who wanted to own more slaves, but approximately five hundred African Americans were relocated to the west.

The Second Seminole War lasted until the early 1840s, but it did not end with the removal of all Seminole to Oklahoma as the U.S. government desired. Instead, the Seminole were victorious—at least to some extent. Approximately four hundred of them remained in their homeland, where many of their descendents still live today.

When the Seminole were driven from their land, the journey to Oklahoma was long and difficult, especially for those who were very young or very old.

Chapter 2

More Triumph and Tears

The year 1855 brought the Third Seminole War to the Indian people remaining in Florida. As more land was opened up to Caucasian settlers, the pressure for Indian removal intensified. While on a trip to Washington to meet President Millard Fillmore in 1852, Billie Bowlegs, a leader of both Seminole and Miccosukees, had indicated that the people he led would leave Florida, but that had not taken place.

The first conflict of the Third Seminole War occurred after a group of soldiers raided Billie Bowlegs' village. In retaliation, the Seminole attacked a survey party containing some of the same men who had stolen materials from their homes. In 1856, General William Harney undertook a campaign of continual pursuit and harassment against the Seminole. Life was already extremely difficult for the Seminole, and several women and children from Billie Bowlegs' camp were captured.

Several months later, in 1858, Bowlegs agreed to meet with a group of

Who Are the Miccosukees?

While many people and the federal government referred to all of the Indian people who were living in Florida as Seminole, many Indian people distinguished themselves from each other in many ways, including where they lived, the language they spoke, and the types of food that they ate. The Seminole who live near Lake Okeechobee speak Muscogee, the language of the Creek people. Other Seminole speak a language now called Miccosukee. They are not the only people who speak Miccosukee, however. There is another group of Indian people who speak Miccosukee living in Southern Florida. They share the history of the Seminole, but since at least the 1920s, some of them have claimed to be a separate tribe. These people were formally recognized as the Miccosukee Tribe by the U.S. government in 1962. There are also several independent Miccosukee-speaking Indians living on or near the Tamiami Trail in Florida. These people do not recognize any agreements that have been made between Indian tribes and the U.S. government. They are staunch traditionalists and continue to claim the rights to much of the land in Florida.

Seminole who had undergone removal. The federal government wanted these men to persuade Bowlegs to join them in the West. Bowlegs was talked into leaving Florida, but other leaders (among them the admired Sam Jones) refused to comply with his decision. Bowlegs and his followers (including several people of African descent) left Florida that same year. This removal brought an end to the Third Seminole War, leaving only an estimated two hundred Seminole still living in their Florida homeland. For the most part, these courageous people maintained a self-imposed isola-tion from European settlers for the next twenty years. The American gov-ernment was soon occupied by the Civil War, and organized harassment of the Florida Seminole ended for a time.

Meanwhile, the Seminole who had been removed to the area of the country that is now Oklahoma were undergoing their own hardships. Imagine what it would be like to be uprooted from your home and tossed onto an unfamiliar foreign land. Think about how you would survive if you had no house in which to live, no stores in which to shop, no money to pay for needed supplies, no garden containing food, and you were not familiar with the wild plants that now surrounded you.

The majority of the Seminole who were relocated to the west arrived between 1836 and 1842. Many of them were actually prisoners of war; they did not come to this new land willingly. Moreover, the federal government had promised aid to the Seminole by providing supplies and even *annuities* to help them get established in their new homeland. However, federal aid was *sporadic,* and sometimes it wasn't received at all. While a number of tribes who had arrived earlier were at least somewhat *acclimated* to their new environment, the Seminole were struggling to adapt without the assistance the U.S. government had promised. To make matters worse, the Seminole were extremely concerned about the safety of the freedpeople who had come to the new territory with them. They had good reason to be

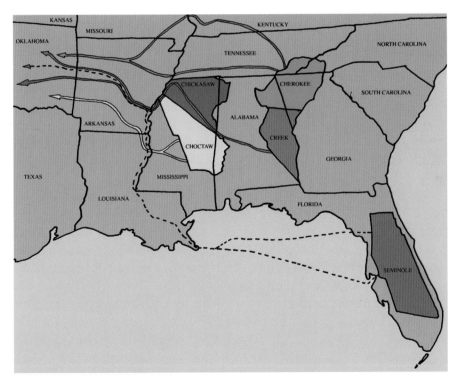

A map showing the "Trail of Tears" taken by several different tribes as they were forced out of their homelands.

afraid because the Creeks, under whose jurisdiction they had been placed, had no concern for the freedom of these people. In fact, they would often kidnap these individuals and sell them to plantation owners. At one point, Chief Holatoochee wrote to Major General Thomas Jessup asking for assistance in dealing with this injustice.

In a ruling that took place in 1849, the Attorney General of the United States ruled that Seminole of African descent were slaves. Instead of turning over their guns as the government and the Creeks ordered, approximately eight hundred people (including John Horse and Wild Cat) left the territory and headed toward Mexico, where slavery had ended in 1829.

After a meeting with President Santa Ana, Wild Cat and the Seminole agreed to patrol the border along the Rio Grand in exchange for pay that included land for farming and homes. In 1851, Wild Cat, John Horse (Juan Caballo), and approximately sixty other Seminole defeated a group of four hundred Texans and Texas Rangers who had crossed the border. When John Horse was later captured and taken to the United States, his friend Wild Cat paid five hundred dollars for his return. When the United States declared that Seminole were independent from the Creek Nation in 1856, some of the Seminole began returning to the western territory, while others stayed with Wild Cat and the "Black Seminole" (Native Americans who were descended from both African Americans and Seminole) in Mexico.

In 1857, an epidemic of smallpox struck the Seminole village, killing many, including Wild Cat. After Wild Cat's death more of his followers returned to the United States, but most of the Black Seminole remained in Mexico until the 1870s.

Slavery had ended in the United States after the Civil War, and the U.S. Army in Texas determined that they were in need of skilled scouts. Chief John Horse and his followers agreed to immigrate to Texas in exchange for food, land, and other necessary supplies. The independent nature of the Seminole exasperated the Army, and it was two years before a suitable leader of the troops was found. Lieutenant John L. Bullis, a Quaker who had joined the military and volunteered to lead black soldiers during the Civil War, soon gained the respect of the Black Seminole scouts. Three of the scouts, Pompey Factor, Issac Payne, and John Ward, received Congressional Medals of Honor for valor after saving Lieutenant Bullis during a battle against Comanches.

Unfortunately, though they waited, hoped, and petitioned the government for three years, the land promised to the Black Seminole was never granted to them. The Army actually reduced their rations to the point where three hundred people had to share food that was only adequate to feed fifty.

The unit of Seminole Scouts was not officially disbanded until the early 1900s, but by that time, many original Black Seminole members had been replaced by other people of African descent from Texas and Mexico and by former U.S. soldiers. The Black Seminole had been moved from one fort to another, but they were never welcomed. Instead, white settlers wanted the land that the Black Seminole farmed. Many, including Chief John Horse, had moved back to Mexico years earlier. Today, descendants of the Black Seminole live on each side of the Rio Grande River.

Meanwhile, in 1843 John Jumper arrived in Oklahoma as a prisoner of the Second Seminole War. Today, a distinction is made between the Seminole Tribe in Florida and the Seminole Nation in Oklahoma. John Jumper served as a member of the Seminole Tribal Council in Oklahoma for many years and eventually became chief of the Seminole Nation there.

It is often said that the Civil War turned brother against brother in the United States. This is also true of the Seminole who were then living in Oklahoma. During the Civil War, they had divided loyalties; some tribal members joined the Union Army while others joined the Confederacy. Because of Union sympathies, some tribe members moved north into Kansas. During this time of unrest, there were two chiefs serving as leaders of the Seminole in the Oklahoma/Kansas area. The chief of the Confederate Seminole was John Jumper. During the war, he achieved the rank of Lieutenant Colonel of the Confederate Army Mounted Seminole Volunteers. Af-

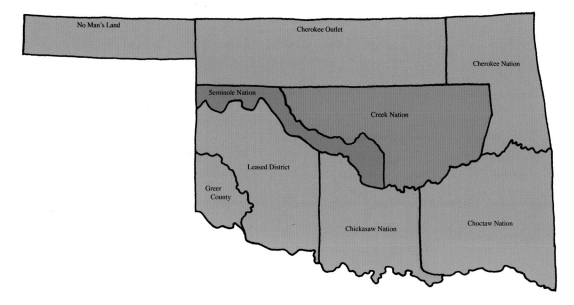

The Seminole's land in Oklahoma appears in green.

ter the war, he served for approximately ten more years as Chief of the Seminole Nation.

While the war raged on, Billie Bowlegs and John (Big John) Chupco, both Town Chiefs, served in the Union Army's Indian Home Guard Brigade. John Chupco became principal chief of the Northern faction of the Seminole Nation.

After the Civil War, the federal government once again turned its attention to the Indians. Never satisfied with the continuing reduction of Indian lands, the government decided to "reorganize" the boundaries of the Oklahoma property. In 1866, the Seminole Nation was required to sign a treaty agreeing to relinquish all of its land to the United States for fifteen cents per acre (a total of $325,362). They then agreed to spend fifty cents per acre to purchase 200,000 acres (81,000 hectares) and a dollar per acre to purchase 175,000 additional acres (70,820 hectares) of land from the Creek Nation. This land was then under the control of the Seminole Nation, but they did grant permission for some white people to live on the property in return for a payment of fifty cents per month.

Elijah Brown, a Caucasian trader, was hired by the federal government to gather the Seminole who had moved to Kansas and transport them back to their new lands in present-day Seminole County, Oklahoma. Brown selected Wewoka (a town that had been founded by Chief John Horse) as the site of the Seminole Nation's capital.

Education of Indian people with a goal toward Christian conversion and assimilation into the Caucasian culture became a new focus for the federal government following the Civil War. Toward that end, a *census* of the Florida Seminole was ordered. The government still hoped to tear these independent people from what was left of their homeland and to relocate them in the West. Lieutenant Richard Henry Pratt, who later established an Indian boarding school in Carlisle, Pennsylvania, was the person charged with surveying the Indian population. He suggested the best way to assim-

A statue depicts the "Unconquered Seminole" as they escape into the Everglades.

ilate the Seminole into American society would be to remove children from the influence of their families and educate them in boarding schools.

After the Civil War and later in the nineteenth century, the hunting, trapping, and trading economy of the Florida Seminole grew as the market for hides and feathers increased. This brought increased contact with trading posts and further influenced the Seminole way of life as trading posts introduced items such as beads, hand-cranked and treadle sewing machines, fabric, trims such as rickrack, watches, and hats into the culture.

Efforts in the early twentieth century to begin draining the Florida Everglades and the building of the Tamiami Trail, a road cutting across the

The Everglades remains a land of mystery and beauty.

A reconstruction of a chickee home.

"river of grass," as the Everglades are sometimes called, exposed once isolated Seminole villages to increasing numbers of outsiders, including developers and tourists. In the face of these challenges, the Seminole, proud and ancient people, continue to maintain their heritage of dignity and freedom.

The tribal flag flies with the American flag, representing the Seminole's sovereignty.

Chapter 3

Current Government

People file into the well-appointed auditorium while television cameras prepare to begin coverage. A reporter is poised to take notes. High-powered executives, attorneys, and elected officials enter, and the regularly scheduled meeting of the Tribal Council of the Seminole Tribe of Florida begins at tribal headquarters, a modern and impressive four-story building located on the Hollywood Reservation. Some of this meeting may be conducted in the tribal language, as the Seminole have carried their strong traditions, including a high regard for both independent thought and consensus of opinion, into the twentieth and twenty-first centuries. Today, the Seminole Tribe of Florida and the Seminole Nation of Oklahoma are completely separate entities. Each has its own constitution and its own government.

The Seminole Tribe of Florida was legally recognized by the U.S. government in 1957, following on the heels of several congressional actions and the Seminole's reaction to them. When a law that allowed Indians to file claims for broken treaties and lost land was passed in 1946, the Seminole filed a claim against the U.S. government within the year. (The case would linger in the courts for thirty years, however. In 1976 the U.S. Indian

Claims Commission decided in favor of the Seminole, but another fourteen years would pass before disputes were settled regarding how the award would be divided between the Seminole Tribe of Florida, the Seminole Nation of Oklahoma, and the Miccosukee Tribe.) Individual Seminole also testified before Congress in 1954 and 1955 concerning the Termination Acts. A congressional effort to eliminate federal responsibility to certain tribes, the Termination Acts were fueled by the desire to reduce federal spending after World War II. For the Florida Seminole, "termination" could have meant being evicted from reservation land.

So, once again, the Seminole were under threat of losing their homes. Services that had been extended to Seminole people by the federal government would have come to an end also. The tribe fought back by organizing and by sending representatives to speak on their behalf before Congress. They asked that federal support and supervision be continued for the next twenty-five years. With vision and foresight, they determined that they would become self-sufficient within those twenty-five years.

Tribal government buildings for the Seminole Tribe of Florida.

Female Leaders

1922 President Warren G. Harding appointed Alice Brown Davis (the daughter of former Chief John F. Brown and Lucy Graybeard, and the granddaughter of former Chief John Jumper) chairman of the Seminole Nation of Oklahoma.

1967 Betty Mae Tiger Jumper was elected chairman of the tribal council of the Seminole Tribe of Florida. She became the first woman elected chairman of an American Indian tribe.

2001 Mary Ann Emarthla was the first woman to be elected assistant chief of the Seminole Nation of Oklahoma.

The people worked together to become a recognized tribe. Money had to be raised for trips to Washington and for other purposes, so lumber and cattle were donated and a rodeo grounds was constructed as a tourist attraction to raise the necessary funds. Because the people did not have a building in which to conduct meetings, they often gathered under a particular tree on the Dania Reservation (later known as the Hollywood Reservation); this tree came to be known as the Council Oak. Newly elected council members are still sometimes welcomed to the council beneath this historic tree.

The Seminole Tribe of Florida was legally recognized when members agreed to develop a government that would operate under a constitution and bylaws based on the laws of the United States. The tribe also agreed to assume legal control of reservation land entrusted to them. Following the centuries-old traditions of the Seminole, which allowed for freedom of speech, the Constitutional Committee was formed, and open meetings and discussions were held on each reservation. A corporate charter was developed, along with the constitution and bylaws, all of which were approved by the U.S. Secretary of the Interior and adopted by a general election involving all adult members of the Florida Seminole.

Elected representatives of each of the Seminole reservations in Florida

Historic Oklahoma Seminole Nation Bands Still Represented on the General Council

Hvteyievlke Band
Thomas Palmer Band
Fushutche Band (Bird Creek)
Tallahassee Band
Tusekia Harjo Band
Dosar Barkus Band (Freedman Band)
Ceasar Bruner Band (Freedman Band)
Nurcup Harjo Band
Ceyvha Band
Hecete Band
Eufaula Band
Ocese Band
Mekusukey Band

now serve on the tribal council, which is the chief governing body and is headed by a chairman and vice chairman. The Seminole Tribe of Florida is a corporation with a board of directors, and each tribal member shares equally in the corporation. The tribal council and the board of directors work together to provide services to tribe members and to diversify the types of businesses and holdings owned and operated by the tribe in an effort to provide security by stabilizing income. The chairman of the tribal council is also the vice president of the board of directors. The president of the board of directors also serves as the vice president of the tribal council. Both the chairman of the tribal council and the president of the board of directors are elected positions. This sharing of offices between governmental bodies effectively links them together. The chairman of the tribal council is the "chief" of the Seminole Tribe of Florida. Seminole Broadcasting, the television station operated by the tribe, provides live coverage of tribal council meetings, so that all members of the tribe can stay informed regarding issues and policies.

Among the duties of the tribal government are the overseeing of money-making ventures of the tribe, such as tribal gaming, cigarette sales, the Ah-Tah-Thi-Ki Museum, and Billie Swamp Safari. The tribal council also watches over the tribe's human resources programs and the Seminole Police Department. The tribe maintains a legal services department, although it does not have a court system. The legal services department oversees the Seminole Utilities Department, Water Resource Management, and a public defender's office. The government of the Seminole Tribe of Florida has definitely led the way toward the economic prosperity that the tribe now enjoys.

To the west, the Seminole Nation of Oklahoma was founded by treaty in

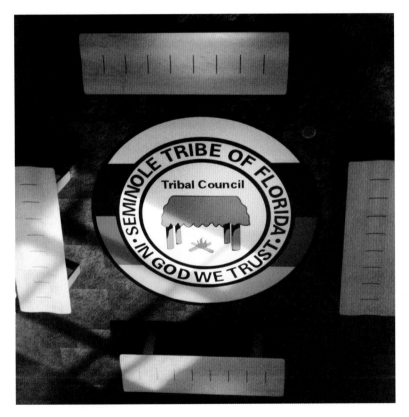

The tribal seal for the Seminole Tribe of Florida.

The Florida Reservations are located at Big Cypress, Hollywood, Brighton, Tampa, and Immokalee (which means "my home" in Miccosukee).

1856. Subsequent treaties, laws, and occurrences that took place as a result of Oklahoma becoming a state and the Oklahoma Indian Welfare Act of 1936 disrupted tribal government, however. Oklahoma had state *segregation* laws that negatively affected the freedmen *faction* of the tribe. The land belonging to the Seminole Tribe became Seminole County and was divided into parcels, which were given to individual tribal members. For a time, tribal chiefs were appointed by the president of the United States, rather than elected by tribe members; that changed when the tribe was reorganized in 1960.

The Seminole Nation of Oklahoma is a *sovereign* nation separate from the Seminole Tribe in Florida. All of the federally recognized Indian tribes are sovereign nations, which means that the U.S. government recognizes them as independent nations located within the United States. They are under the protection of the United States, but they have many independent rights, including the right to conduct business and make laws (as long as they do not interfere with the laws of the United States). According to the tribal constitution of the Seminole Nation of Oklahoma, its governmental powers are divided into three distinct departments: *legislative*, *executive*, and *judicial*, just like the U.S. government.

The Hollywood Reservation's tribal offices.

Former Chairmen of the Seminole Tribe of Florida and Highlights of Their Terms of Office

1957–1967   Billy Osceola
Schools in Florida were desegregated during Chairman Osceola's administration, so one of the things he focused on was to encourage Seminole to take advantage of increased educational opportunities. The tribe began to earn money by leasing lands during this administration. They also opened the Okalee arts and crafts village.

1967–1971   Betty Mae Tiger Jumper
As a registered nurse, Chairman Jumper was especially concerned about tribal health and social services issues. When President Nixon called for increasing independence for tribes, Chairman Jumper's administration passed a resolution indicating its desire to direct their own tribal programs involving social service issues as well as education and employment opportunities and the tribe's cattle program. Chairman Jumper also recognized the value of unity among tribal nations and was one of the founders of the United South and Eastern Tribes (USET).

1971–1979   Howard Tommie
Chairman Tommie was an advocate of the 1975 Indian Self-Determination Act and the 1976 Indian Health Care Improvement Act. Under his leadership, the Seminole opened tax-free smoke shops, which sold cigarettes, and successfully fought a legal challenge from the State of Florida that questioned the Seminole's right to earn money in this manner. With federal aid, health clinics were opened, Head Start was initiated for young children, educational programs for elementary school children were expanded, and housing and recreational programs were developed. A number of jobs that had formerly been handled by the Bureau of Indian Affairs became the responsibility of the tribe.

1979–2003   James E. Billie
A focus of Chairman Billie's administration was sovereignty and the right of independent decision-making that it granted to the tribe. The Seminole's first bingo hall was opened during Chairman Billie's administration, and it soon became the largest income-producing venture of the tribe. The tribe successfully fought two years of court challenges that questioned its right to operate the facility. In 1993, the tribe was able to pay off a debt to the federal government that it had incurred during formation of the tribe and take over the funding of several programs.

Lighthorsemen

The Seminole Nation of Oklahoma still uses the historic term "lighthorsemen" to refer to members of its police force. Today's lighthorsemen are cross-deputized so that they are also members of the Seminole County Police Department.

While the Seminole Nation of Oklahoma does not have a reservation, it does own tribal land. Tribal offices are located on tribal land in Wewoka, Oklahoma. Chief Kenneth Chambers was elected principal chief in 2001; he has the honor of being the twenty-second chief of the Seminole Nation. One of his duties as principal chief is to preside over meetings of the General Council, which is the Seminole Nation's governing body. The General Council is composed of twenty-eight elected members who meet quar-

The Seminole Nation of Oklahoma has its own police force.

John Jumper, former Chief of the Seminole Nation of Oklahoma, died in 1896. When speaking of his death, Chief Pashmataha of the Choctaws said it was "like the fall of a mighty tree in the stillness of the forest."

terly—or more often when necessary—in the Council House, which is owned and maintained by the Seminole Nation. The General Council oversees matters pertaining to employment, economic development, and social programs regarding the Seminole Nation. Also serving in her present office since 2001, Mary Ann Emarthla is the first woman to be elected assistant chief.

The General Council is composed of two members from each of the fourteen Seminole bands (or family groups), including two freedmen bands composed of descendants of former slaves who found refuge among the Seminole. Originally there were twenty-five Seminole family bands that moved from Florida to Oklahoma. The number was reduced during the Civil War and then further reduced until only fourteen bands remain in Oklahoma today. In the late 1800s, the General Council was composed of forty-two members, because the *mekko*, a leader who sometimes provided counseling or presided over meetings and celebrations, of each of the fourteen bands was also a member. The Seminole are historically a **matriarchal** society, so by virtue of inheritance, individuals belong to the same bands as their mothers. Each band elects its own chairman and vice chairman and conducts a monthly meeting to discuss tribal matters.

According to Assistant Chief Emarthla, gaming and federal funds, ad-

Colors on the tribal seal of the Seminole Tribe of Florida are the same as the traditional Seminole medicine colors: yellow represents security or serenity, red represents blood or war, black represents mourning, and white represents purity.

ministered through the **Bureau of Indian Affairs**, are the largest sources of income for the Seminole Nation. Income is also generated by the TAG Office, which has the authority to issue Seminole Nation license plates and register automobiles belonging to tribe members. Only enrolled tribe members are allowed to purchase these plates. Tribe members have the option to purchase regular Oklahoma state license plates, but when they purchase plates from the tribe, three percent of the registration fee goes to the state, and the rest of the money becomes available to the tribe to use as it sees fit.

Tourism brings revenue to the Seminole reservations in Florida.

The Seminole Nation generates funds by issuing license plates to tribe members.

In the past, mekkos, *tastanaks* (respected warriors), **clan elders**, and **medicine men** and women were among the individuals who established and maintained the Seminole government. They have left a strong legacy within the written constitutions, government positions, and governmental duties of the Seminole Tribes.

Seminole spirituality is closely linked to their sense of connection to God and the Earth.

Chapter 4

Spiritual Beliefs

Seminole are a spiritual people who have had a unique belief in God (sometimes referred to as Breathmaker) for many centuries. *Oral history* has been the method for passing spiritual stories from one generation to another. Traditional stories about creation can differ from one person and one clan to the next.

A member of the bird clan might explain the story of creation this way:

When God created the earth the Seminole were under the ground, but they wanted to come out. God made a garden and planted seeds in it. As the seeds grew they began to make a hole in the earth. The bird clan was able to peck at the hole and make it larger. As soon as the hole was large enough, the bird clan flew out from under the ground. Other clans came out of the hole after the bird clan.

People from different clans have different ideas about which clan came upon the earth first. Another creation story explains that seven clans were born out of the backbone of Mother Earth. In this *rendition,* the clans were again in the ground, but this time the mountains opened up and the wind

> Sofke is a traditional Seminole drink made from corn.

clan *emerged* first. The panther came out second, and after that the deer; the others followed.

In yet another tale of creation, God is the Grandfather who creates all animals, puts them into a shell, and then places it along the earth's backbone. After a long time, the roots of a tree that is growing beside the shell make a crack in it. God had already told the panther to come out first, but the wind starts to move around the crack and make it larger. Just when it looks like the wind will escape first, it grabs the panther and helps him get out first. In this version, the bird again pecks at the crack to make it larger, but this time, the bird is the second to emerge. The rest of the animals follow—but in this creation story, thousands of animals emerge to populate the earth. God observes the animals without intervention, which may imply that although God is the Creator and set the earth in motion, He does not desire to always actively control what happens on it. According to this story, God

Fire often plays a central role in Native ceremonies. The Seminole built a fire composed of logs radiating out from a central point. As the ends of the logs burned, they were pushed toward the center in order to maintain the fire.

Seminole Religious Words

Muscogee	English
Hesaketv emese	Breathmaker (used in hymns and biblical translations to mean Jesus Christ or God)
hvlwe tvlofv	high town (heaven)
totkvrakko	big fire (hell)

put the animals into clans and assigned certain qualities and duties to them after they had been *dispersed* upon the earth. For example, the panther clan received knowledge to make medicine and laws.

. Like other spiritual people, the Seminole developed ceremonies and celebrations that brought unity to the tribe and marked special seasons and occasions of life. Some of them are still observed by *traditionalists* today.

The use of corn was important in the Seminole culture, and the most important annual traditional celebration is the Green Corn Dance. The four-day ceremony of renewal is held in late spring or early summer. Crops are planted several months prior to the event, so by the time of the ceremony, new corn and other foods are available. Many North American Indian tribes have similar celebrations, which are conducted to give thanks to God the Creator for the gift of food.

The Green Corn Dance is a very private Seminole occasion, and very few non-Indians have ever witnessed it. Let's imagine a Green Corn Dance as it may have been a century ago, while remembering that modern versions may have changed considerably. This is a special event, and people will dress in their finest clothing for it.

In addition to performing certain *rituals*, Seminole who did not often see each other because they lived many miles apart took this opportunity to come together in order to exchange ideas and socialize, even though women and men remained separate for much of the event.

You might not know where to set up camp as you entered the celebration area. If that was the case, you approached the man in charge and told

The number four has special significance in many Indian traditions. For example, a family will mourn for four days following the death of a family member. On the fourth day they will drink or wash with special herbs, and widows will continue to mourn for four moons. The herbs for mourning will have been obtained from a medicine man or medicine woman. Medicine men and medicine women are important spiritual leaders who still have an active role in Seminole life today.

him your clan. He would then explain where you should set up your camp. Specific activities would take place on each of the four days of the Green Corn Dance ceremony. Much of the first day would be spent setting up clan camps and gathering wood. The central fire is a very important part of many American Indian ceremonies, as is dancing.

The Green Corn Dance celebration involved many hours of *stomp dancing*. During some of these ceremonial dances, women wore turtle-shell rattles and kept the beat as they did a sort of shuffle step. Whether or not you were allowed to participate in specific dances depended on your age and sex. Many of the dances were performed only by adult male members of the tribe.

The second day of the ceremony usually involved the building or repair of the main building. It was also a day of feasting in preparation for the next day's fast. Stickball, which is played with a sort of racket, is a traditional part of Seminole culture and was played as part of this annual event. At the Green Corn Dance there would be a very exciting game—the women would play against the men. Disputes between members of the community were sometimes settled with a game of stickball as well.

The discussion of legal matters and the judging and punishment of crimes that had taken place during the previous year were an important part of the traditional proceedings. Disagreements among tribe members would also be *reconciled* at this time. Another game of stickball might be played, and dances would usually be held in the afternoon. This year, a feather dance would be performed, and it was the responsibility of the Bird Clan. Only men participated in this particular dance, which involved the use of long poles that were decorated on top with feathers. The dance was so enjoyable that it would be performed several times during the day. Other years it might not be performed at all.

Everyone watched as the "medicine fire" was lit on the third day by a medicine man, who used a special piece of flint kept in a *medicine bundle*. This fire was used to relight all the clan fires, which had been extinguished in preparation for this ceremonial lighting.

As a symbol of *purification*, all the men of the tribe would vomit following the drinking of an *emetic* on this day. Young boys would not take part in this event or in the fasting that followed, but they were scratched on the arms and legs because bleeding was also a sign of the purification.

Another exciting part of the Green Corn ceremony was the bestowing of adult names on the boys. If you were a boy of the proper age, you might have been waiting in anticipation for this important event. Clan elders decided on these names prior to the Green Corn Dance, and usually names of deceased members of the tribe were used for this purpose. The naming ceremony took place in the evening after a period of social drinking.

By this time you have noticed that most men have scratched bodies, and

Big Cypress First Baptist Church was the first Christian church to be built on the Big Cypress Reservation.

those unscratched would be scratched on the fourth day. They would also gather together and take part in a sweat bath. Pouring the remainder of the purification drink over heated rocks created the needed steam. The men would bathe in water following the sweat bath, and the women would prepare the meal that ended the men's fast. You felt happy and excited as new corn was served with other food to mark the end of this important four-day event. The final evening would be spent dancing and telling stories all night long.

The Seminole people maintain many of their traditions (like the Green Corn Dance), but most details concerning them are considered private and even sacred. As such, they are not usually discussed with people who are not members of the tribe.

Seminole who were forced to **emigrate** from Florida to Oklahoma brought their traditions, including the Green Corn Dance, with them. People lived in separate bands (also called *etvlwv* or tribal towns). These were often composed of six or more clans who shared a ceremonial center area

A museum display shows the influence of Native traditions on early Seminole churches.

The Lord's Prayer

Muscogee	English
Pu´rke hvlwe liketskat, ce hocefkvt vcakekvs. Cem ohmekketvt vlvkekvs. Mimv hvlwe nake kometske momat etvpomet yvmv ekvnvn oh momekvs.	Our Father which art in heaven, Hallowed be thy name. Thy kingdom come. Thy will be done in earth, as it is in heaven.
Nettv vrahkv tvkliken mucv nettvn pu´mvs.	Give us this day our daily bread.
Momet pum ahuervn es pum wikvs, vhuericeyat es em wikakeyat, etvpomen.	And forgive us our debts, as we forgive our debtors.
Nake pu naorkepuece taye eskerretv `sep oh ahyetskvs; momis holwakat a sepu´ssisvs. Ohmekketvt, yekcetvt, momen rakketvt cenake emunkvt omekv. Emen.	And lead us not into temptation, but deliver us from evil: for thine is the kingdom, and the power, and the glory, forever. Amen

and sacred fire. Each group had a mekko. Clans came together for stomp dances and other traditional rituals at ceremonial grounds. Traditionalists still conduct these activities in the area.

By the mid- to late 1800s, however, Christianity had also become a part of life for many Oklahoma Seminole, largely through the efforts of the Southern Baptist Convention Home Mission Board. Several other **denominations,** including Methodists, Catholics, and Presbyterians, sent missionaries to try to convert the Seminole, but none were as successful as the Baptists.

Not everyone who promoted Christianity did so for honorable reasons. Some people used Christianity as a tool for assimilation of Indian people

Jack M. Schultz, an assistant professor of anthropology at Concordia University, has conducted an extensive study of historic Seminole Baptist churches in Oklahoma. In his book, *The Seminole Baptist Churches of Oklahoma*, Professor Schultz states that there were at least three things that may have made the Baptist faith appealing to Seminole people:

1. Congregational independence (which he says allowed the Seminole to structure their churches in new and unique ways)
2. Congregations were allowed to select and train their own pastors
3. Congregations and individuals were allowed to have a broad interpretation of scripture and belief

Today there are more than fifty Seminole and Creek churches in Oklahoma.

into American society. Many times, if the mekko of a town **converted**, one or more clans or even the entire town would also convert. Sometimes the mekko would become the pastor.

Chief John Jumper, for example, became a pastor, and in 1850, he designed and built the Spring Baptist Church with his son-in-law, Governor John F. Brown. This is one of the oldest churches in Oklahoma, and services are still held there. When John Jumper declined reelection as chief of the Seminole Nation in 1877, it was because he wanted to spend more time doing missionary work.

In 1871, the Methodist Conference of Florida sent a missionary to work among the Florida Seminole, but the independent Seminole resisted conversion. Later missionaries were more successful, and in the 1890s, an Episcopal church was established on Big Cypress. The first Baptist church was dedicated on the Dania (now Hollywood) Reservation in 1936. By 1946, Seminole men were studying to become ministers at the Florida Baptist Institute. Today several Baptist churches exist on the Florida reservations.

According to Professor Jack Schultz, who has conducted extensive research regarding Seminole Baptist churches, the churches in Oklahoma and Florida are quite different from each other since they arose in different locations under different circumstances. Schultz identified several Baptist churches and **outbuildings** in rural Oklahoma settings that had **configura-**

Stickball played a central role in Seminole spiritual celebrations.

tions similar to each other. Each church faced east and had an attached *arbor* where services could be held in hot weather. A road circled around the church and arbor, and several camp houses, which could serve as residences during long services, were placed along the road. Many of these church grounds also include a cleared area in the woods (often with two benches) for more private prayer. Cemeteries are usually located near the church grounds. The churches' interiors have a common configuration with the pews being placed along the *perimeter*. According to Schultz, the outside and inside configurations of these churches may have been influenced by the traditional layout of Indian ceremonial grounds.

Tradition, spirituality, and religion have always been part of Seminole culture, and they continue to play an important role in people's lives. Although most modern-day Seminole in both Florida and Oklahoma are Christians, they have not forgotten their ancient ceremonies and oral traditions.

Many services are offered at the Hollywood Reservation's tribal offices.

Chapter 5

Social Structures Today

Historically, Seminole were agriculturalists. They grew corn, beans, squash, and potatoes, and they raised horses, chickens, and cattle. Families ate meals together, but if visitors stopped by—and at ceremonies such as the Green Corn Dance—men and boys ate first, while women and girls ate later. In the past, few opportunities for education existed and those that did exist were mainly at Indian boarding schools. In the early 1940s, only five Seminole people in Florida graduated from high school. Clan membership played an important role in the everyday life of many Seminole.

Tremendous changes took place for the Seminole during the twentieth century. They established a new government and opened businesses. Tribal economics developed and grew. However, even today many of the best things about the past remain the same. Some tribe members are farmers and cattle ranchers, for example. But many exciting opportunities for education and employment now exist.

Indians no longer have to leave their families and go away to boarding schools in order to obtain an education. In the 1940s, school on Big Cypress was conducted in a chickee, and children could only attend until the fourth grade. Today, 151 students on Big Cypress attend beautiful Ahfachkee School, from pre-kindergarten through the twelfth grade. Ahfachkee, meaning "to be happy," was the name of the land before the school was built upon it. It is also an appropriate name, because great things are happening in this modern and well-appointed school with its comfortable library and computers in every classroom.

In the past, the federal government used schools to destroy Indian culture. Children in Indian boarding schools were not allowed to speak their native languages, to wear their hair in traditional ways, or to wear traditional clothing. Today, however, the Ahfachkee School celebrates Seminole

Many social services for families are available through the modern and beautiful Family Investment Center on Big Cypress. The Cultural Center, Learning Resources, and other offices are also housed here.

The Seminole are a matriarchal society where clan membership is passed to children through their mother. Individuals are not supposed to marry within their own clan. Most of the eight Florida Seminole family clans are named after animals. The clan names are Bird, Panther, Deer, Otter, Bear, Snake, Wind, and Bigtown. Some former clans, such as the alligator clan, are now extinct.

Women cooked, watched after children, took care of their gardens, and maintained the camp. Men were warriors and protectors; that's why they sometimes walked in front of women.

culture. Tribal history and traditional arts are taught, along with the Miccosukee language. Less than six years ago, the school's national test scores were low, the dropout rate was high, and the federal government considered taking over administration of the school. The Seminole Tribe of Florida was able to turn all of that around, and in 2000, Ahfachkee School was awarded a Title I Distinguished School Award. With generous funding and support from the community, Ahfachkee School is able to employ one teacher for every eight students. By doing this, each student is guaranteed the individual attention and instruction that he or she may need. One of Ahfachkee's goals is to prepare students to attend the best colleges in the United States, and they are reaching that goal.

Not all Seminole children attend Ahfachkee School; more than five hundred attend public schools in Florida, and over seventy are enrolled in various universities and colleges. When children of the Seminole Tribe of Florida are accepted into college, their families don't have to worry about how they will pay for it. The tribe believes in the saying "It takes a village to raise a child." They provide incentives for attendance and achievement throughout elementary and high school, and when a child is admitted to college, the tribe accepts responsibility for the cost.

The Seminole Tribe of Florida has an educational division that delivers many educational services to tribe members from the time they are six weeks old through when they become senior citizens. More than 90 percent of tribe members take advantage of these programs. For example, each reservation has a Parents Advisory Committee, and two members of each of these committees are on the Education Advisory Board. This program has something for everyone—from preschool, **Head Start**, and **early intervention** programs for children with special needs, to **GED** programs for those who didn't finish high school but now wish to do so. Adult education programs allow people to improve skills in subjects ranging from language arts to personal budgeting. Tribe members can even request educational programs in topics of special interest to them. Educational counseling is provided on all of the reservations. Vocational training is also offered. The tribe participates in the Florida Governor's Council on Indian Affairs Summer Youth Program, where teenagers between the ages of fourteen and seventeen attend a two-week program at Florida State University that allows them to gain a college experience while exploring career opportunities. The educational division also provides an after-school tutoring program for elementary and high school students and a summer employment program for students who are between fourteen and seventeen years old.

Only fifty years ago, indoor plumbing was uncommon in tribal homes.

The Seminole Nation operates a food distribution program.

Libraries operated by the tribe are located on each of the three major reservations of the Seminole Tribe of Florida.

Many families still lived in chickees. Now there are many opportunities for employment on the reservations, houses are modern, and home ownership is a possibility for everyone. By 1962, the Seminole Tribe of Florida had a revolving credit program that made home loans to qualified tribal families. Today, through the Seminole Housing Authority, tribe members can rent tribally owned houses, or they can go before the Land Use Committee and request permission to build a home on one of the reservations. Those who do build on one of the reservations may only sell their homes to another member of the Seminole Tribe.

Tribe members have the ability to become business owners too. If they want to operate a business on one of the reservations, they can go before a committee and request a loan. Of course they also have the freedom to apply for loans from banks or other lenders off the reservation. A business that is on the reservation cannot be sold to someone outside the tribe.

Many services are available to people living on the reservations, including police and emergency management (ambulances) and a volunteer fire

Fifty years ago, many Seminole in Florida lived in chickees or homes like this display at Billy Swamp Safari. Today, most have modern, comfortable homes.

department. Medical clinics are also operated on reservations for members of the Seminole Tribe who need health services. The *Seminole Tribune*, an award-winning newspaper, keeps people aware of all local events, as does Seminole Broadcasting, a cable television channel that allows even home-bound tribe members to watch tribal council meetings as well as sports events and other programs of interest. The Seminole Tribe of Florida also conducts special programs for tribe members who are senior citizens.

The Seminole Nation of Oklahoma has a long history of boarding schools for its children. Unfortunately, these schools were operated during

Nora Deere is a Community Health Service worker. One of the major services provided by the Community Health Service is transportation for health needs. Workers also make home visits and refer tribe members to other tribal programs as needed.

the time when Indian children were placed in boarding schools in order to remove them from their parents' influence and deprive them of their culture. Oak Ridge Mission, the first school for Seminole, was established by the Presbyterian Church in 1843. John Bemo, a nephew of Osceola, was in charge of the school. Oak Ridge Mission was abandoned before the Civil War and replaced by Ramsey Mission, which was located near Wewoka. Sasakwa, a school for girls, was built in 1880 near the present-day city of Seminole. The Mekasukey Mission Academy was established under the leadership of Governor John F. Brown for Seminole and Creek boys in 1891. Mekasukey Mission was in session nine months out of the year. In addition to attending classes, students raised vegetables along with animals for meat and dairy products.

In 1894, Emahaka Academy was established by the Seminole Nation for the education of the girls of the tribe, and it merged with the Sasakwa school. Emahaka was an exact replica of Mekasukey Mission. A broad number of subjects were taught at Emahaka, ranging from arithmetic to foreign languages and natural philosophy. Alice Brown Davis, who would later be appointed chairman of the Seminole Nation, was the superintendent of Emahaka Mission in 1908. By 1930, both Emahaka Academy and Meka-

Head Start offers Seminole children the enrichment programs they need to thrive.

The Seminole are working to provide quality education to their young people. Ahfachkee is an award-winning school.

sukey Academy were closed, and Mekasukey Mission Academy's buildings later burned down. Today, Seminole children in Oklahoma attend local public schools, but in some schools, as many as 90 percent of the students are Indian.

The Seminole Nation has two Head Start programs that are available for preschool-aged children, and beginning elements of the Muscogee language are taught there. Four day care centers are operated for children of parents who are in school or working. These programs are funded by the Department of Health and Human Services. Another part of this program will pay a relative to care for a child whose parent is in school or working. REACH is a wellness program that the tribe administers for school children. Obesity is one of the issues that are addressed. Activities such as walking, swimming, and aerobics are provided as a way of promoting health. Basketball is also sponsored in the evenings for adults.

The Seminole Nation directs its own Indian Child Welfare Program. The goal is to try to keep children with family members or with foster parents who are tribal members. The Seminole want to keep Indian children in Native American homes whenever possible in order to maintain the culture.

The Seminole Nation administers many social programs. For example, the Housing Authority Program helps low-income people make needed repairs to their homes. Some tribe members also receive assistance to pay utility expenses. The Older Americans Program provides day activities, including exercise, special events, and trips for tribal elders. Typical trips include one taken to attend a Christmas Tree Festival.

The Seminole Nation in Oklahoma now has a modern *dialysis* center, which is available to the paying members of the general public as well as to members of the tribal community.

The Communications Department of the Seminole Nation of Oklahoma produces the tribal newsletter, *Cokv Tvlvme*, which is published monthly. *Cokv Tvlvme* is widely distributed among tribe members, including many who live out of state. The *Cokv Tvlvme* is a way for off-reservation tribe members to keep in contact with the tribe and to make sure that they are informed of tribal matters.

The Herman Osceola Gymnasium is across the road from Ahfachkee School, which makes it convenient for student use.

Beverly Streeter is in charge of Higher Education and Adult Education Programs for the Seminole Nation of Oklahoma.

The social structures of today's Seminole people are far more diverse and intricate than they were in the days when the clans were the dominant social structure. The Seminole have done a good job at adapting to the modern world while maintaining their ties to the past.

Fabric arts are a vital demonstration of Seminole creativity.

Chapter 6

Traditional and Contemporary Art

Tiny lizards dart along the smooth railing ahead of your hand. Moisture drips from bromeliads and other tropical plants along the raised wooden trail. Birds call a greeting to each other from the treetops. You see a group of chickees ahead in a clearing, and you realize you have reached your destination—the Seminole camp of the Ah-tah-thi-ki Museum on the Big Cypress Reservation.

The word *Ah-tah-thi-ki* means "to learn," and today we learn that the traditional artistic objects of the Seminole are timeless. Exquisite examples are still being created here in the museum village and in Seminole homes, although the number of artists making them is dwindling.

Wild sweet grass is still being handpicked in the higher areas of the Everglades and dried in the sun. Skilled basket makers then wind the *aromatic* fiber in distinctive shapes and stitch the coiled layers together with colorful *embroidery* thread using decorative stitches. More thread is some-

The artwork of Gary Montgomery captures a sense of Native spirituality.

times used to add additional decorative elements to baskets. Some baskets have lids and others are open. Seminole artists have been making sturdy sweet grass baskets in various styles and in many different sizes for more than sixty years.

The Seminole have also made creative use of thread and cloth since they first obtained them through trade with Europeans. The Seminole's most **renowned** artistic use of these materials is in the production of patchwork clothing, which probably began among the Miccosukee-speaking Seminole at about the time of World War I.

Of course the Seminole people did not always have the luxury of time and stability that is needed to make handcrafted objects. Three wars forced them to live a nomadic lifestyle. Entire camps often needed to be abandoned quickly, and people were not always able to carry possessions with them. Nevertheless, Seminole women were able to develop their skills as seamstresses a hundred years prior to the appearance of Seminole patchwork. This ability is displayed in paintings such as the one of Chief Tukose Emaathla, painted in 1826. The portrait documents the use of *appliqué*, which is different than patchwork. Patchwork involves sewing cut fabric strips or other shapes to each other, and appliqué is the sewing of one piece of fabric on top of another. It is unlikely that Seminole people made patchwork before they had sewing machines.

Although we do not know exactly when Seminole made the first patchwork garments, we do know that by the early 1890s, an increasing number of Seminole were purchasing hand-cranked sewing machines. The introduction of the sewing machine opened new opportunities for artistic expression in cloth. It also allowed work to be completed faster, so more elaborate designs could be accomplished in a much shorter amount of time. By World War I, Seminole patchwork was seen in *exhibition villages*. Today, people make patchwork clothing for sale, for personal use, and for competitions that take place at tribal fairs and *powwows*. Typically, rows of patchwork are interspersed with rows of solid colored fabric. Many patch-

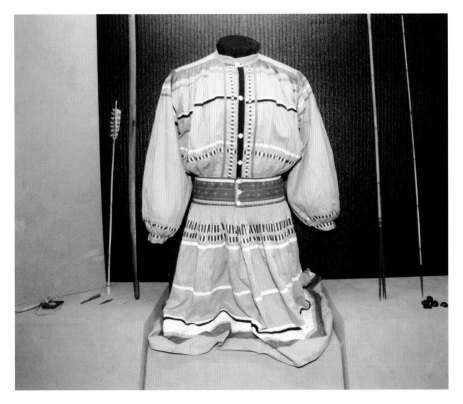

An early example of Seminole sewing.

Traditional and Contemporary Art 67

The first documented Seminole use of a sewing machine appeared in an 1881 report to the Smithsonian by Reverend Clay MacCauley. Reverend MacCauley reported use of the machine by a man known both as Me-le and John Willis Mikko. Within ten years other reports of Seminole women and men using sewing machines appeared.

work variations are now used, and names such as rain, turtle, and arrow have been assigned to identify many of them. In addition to the common forms, some individuals develop their own unique patterns. While Seminole patchwork is almost totally exclusive to clothing, at least one well-known artist, Effie Osceola, has made several large patchwork panels **on commission**. One series of four panels is entitled *Rain, Lightning, Storm, and Fire*. Each of the panels in this series measures an impressive five feet by ten feet (1.5 meters by 3 meters).

Possibly because of the need to live a **transient** lifestyle, the Seminole do not have a history of decorative pottery making as do some of the other North American Indian tribes. They do, however, have a history of finger-weaving—which was used to make straps—and beadwork—which was used to make such things as embroidered **bandolier** bags. Later, loomed beadwork was used instead of fingerweaving. While items like bandoliers may be made today for clothing competitions, the more common types of contemporary beaded items include small objects such as hair clips, watchbands, and jewelry made for the tourist trade.

Cloth dolls stuffed with **palmetto** became a favorite souvenir to purchase from the Seminole early in the twentieth century, and it is still a favorite to-day. Prior to the 1900s, crude dolls were sometimes carved from wood for children. The cloth dolls of the twentieth and now twenty-first century were originally developed specifically to sell to tourists. They have become well-known as Seminole art, however, and are prized by collectors. The dolls are dressed in patchwork clothing, which is representative of that traditionally worn by the Seminole. Dolls are widely available in a variety of sizes and price ranges, so even people with a strict budget can become art collectors. Generally speaking, the larger the doll and the more elaborate the patchwork clothing, the more expensive it will be. Some baskets are

Today's Seminole still create bright and intricate fabric patterns.

Learn Miccosukee	
Miccosukee	English
taweekaache	design (used to refer to patchwork)

now made with dolls attached to the top of them.

Noah Billie was a contemporary Seminole artist who expressed himself as a painter. Mr. Billie, who died in the year 2000, had a unique style, and his paintings are a tribute to Seminole life and culture. Many of his works are at the Ah-tah-thi-ki Museum. (You can view them at www.seminoletribe.com/calendar/dna/noah/paintings.shtml.)

If you visit the Seminole Nation Museum in Wewoka, Oklahoma, you can tour a display containing paintings and sculptures by many contemporary Native American artists. Notable among them are works by Seminole painter Gary Montgomery, who was born in Shawnee, Oklahoma. He has the distinction of being a member of the Masters Category of the Five Civilized Tribes Museum, which is located in Muskogee, Oklahoma. His paintings capture spiritual and mystical aspects of Native American culture. He

A sweet grass basket handmade by the Seminole.

Enoch Kelly Haney's sculpture, Universal Man.

has won many awards for his work, including the 1995 President's Award at the Red Earth Native American Cultural Festival. Montgomery's paintings have been exhibited in Europe and Japan as well as across America.

If you visit the state capitol building in Oklahoma City you will see a twenty-three-foot tall (seven meters) bronze warrior standing atop the capitol dome. Called *The Guardian*, this impressive statue is the work of Seminole/Creek artist Enoch Kelly Haney. The warrior carries a spear.

Traditional and Contemporary Art   71

The spiritual importance of the pipe is reflected in this work by Gary Montgomery.

Haney explains, "When a Native American warrior was threatened by overwhelming odds, he would drive his lance into the ground. He staked himself to the ground to show he was standing his ground." He says that *The Guardian* symbolizes the people who have helped him in his life, such as his family and teachers, the members of his church, and the residents of his district. (He mentions his district because, in addition to being one of the most talented artists in North America, Haney is also a former Oklahoma State Senator.) Now the state of Oklahoma has the distinction of being the only state in the nation with a statue representing a Native American atop its capitol dome.

When the state decided to place a work of art on the structure, they had a contest to select the artist who would make the work and offered a prize of $50,000 to the winner. Those who wanted to participate sent in their ideas. A group of judges selected the winner without knowing who the individual artists were. When Senator Haney's work was selected, he declined the $50,000 prize. He gave the money back to the state and explained, "We want the statue to be a gift to Oklahoma from our family. It's a way of saying thanks to others who have helped us."

Enoch Kelly Haney is also recognized as a Master Artist of the Five Civilized Tribes. His smaller sculptures and paintings are on exhibition at the Seminole Nation Museum. The works of this internationally recognized and generous artist have been widely exhibited in Europe and Asia as well as in the United States.

The Seminole in Florida are working to preserve the beauty of their land.

Chapter 7

Accomplishments and Contributions to the World

Sometimes going to school seems like a chore. You might look out the classroom window and think about how nice it would be to go outside. The teacher may assign a book to be read that holds little interest for you. But what would life be like if you could not read and desperately wanted to know what secrets were written between the tantalizing covers of a glossy magazine? Imagine how you would feel if you wanted to go to school, but the schools near your home closed their doors to you.

Betty Mae Tiger grew up knowing what that feels like. When she was a young Seminole girl in the 1930s, schools were segregated, and neither the local school for white children nor the one for black children would allow her to attend. In order to go to school and learn how to read, Betty Mae had to leave the love and security of her family and move to another state far from home. Imagine how difficult it must have been to make that decision to move forward, but Betty Mae and her parents did so when she was just fourteen. By doing so, she took the first courageous step in a life that would be marked with important milestones for herself and for the Seminole people.

Betty Mae attended Cherokee Indian Boarding School run by the Quakers in North Carolina. While there, she adapted quickly to new foods and new habits. She attended classes and learned to read, but her world expanded in many other ways, too. She was introduced to snow, learned how to do the *jitterbug*, and even learned to drive a tractor!

While on a summer vacation in Florida, Betty Mae again courageously faced segregation. When the cook at a local restaurant refused to serve her at the counter and became verbally abusive, Betty Mae stood her ground with this adult man and sternly explained to him that she would return and he *would* serve her. Betty Mae had become the friend of an influential woman, and after hearing about Betty Mae's experience, this woman took

Tourists on Big Cypress reservation have an opportunity to see firsthand the wonders of the Everglades.

Although it was not composed strictly of Seminole, Company C of the 279th Battalion was one of the all-Indian units of the famous Fighting 45th Division that fought in World War II. Many Native Americans have served in the armed forces.

Betty Mae to see the mayor. When Betty Mae was again refused service at the store, her friends were there to witness it, and the mayor threatened to close the establishment if the cook continued to refuse service to Indian people. The man served Betty Mae.

Betty Mae's grandmother had taught her that when you set a goal for yourself you must complete it. Learning to read and graduating from school were two of the first goals that Betty Mae accomplished, but many more were to follow. She decided that she wanted to become a nurse and provide health care to the Seminole. Once again, she had to leave her family in order to fulfill her dream while she attended Kiowa Teaching Hospital in Oklahoma.

After she graduated and began to work as a nurse among the Seminole, she sometimes had to do so with courage. Modern highways didn't exist, and travel to isolated locations was difficult. Many people were skeptical of modern medicine and resentful of anything they interpreted as an intrusion on their lives and traditions. But Betty Mae *persevered*, and most people began to appreciate the benefits she and another field nurse brought to them. Betty Mae loved her work so much that she continued to do it from 1947 until 1964, either on the road or in the clinic, even when government funds for her pay sometimes ran out. Her Seminole patients had a special name for her—Doctor Lady.

Betty Mae married Moses Jumper in 1946. Always enterprising, she sometimes made crafts to sell to tourists, but in 1947 she realized that she could make more money from tourists in another way—Betty Mae became an alligator wrestler!

Political ambitions were the last thing on her mind in the 1950s when the Seminole Tribe learned of the government's desire to terminate its responsibility toward them. Yet, when the Seminole Indian committee was formed to deal with the situation, Betty Mae was elected secretary—and her political life began. Her skills as an interpreter were used often in those days, and in 1957 (and again in 1959), she was elected vice chairman of the tribal council. As busy as she was, Betty Mae still took an active interest in the education of Seminole children. She even acted as an unofficial truant officer, sometimes driving through cow pastures to collect wayward children and return them to school! She was also a visiting teacher on one of the reservations and a member of the Seminole Tribe of Florida, Inc.'s Board of Directors.

In 1961, Betty Mae became one of the cofounders and coeditors (with Alice Osceola, then a senior in high school) of the *Seminole Indian News*, a monthly newspaper operated as a private enterprise. The newspaper was unique in that it tried to represent both the Miccosukee and the Seminole viewpoints on various matters. It was free of censorship and brought needed information to Seminole people during a critical time for tribal government and businesses.

Betty Mae was elected a representative to the tribal council of the Dania (now Hollywood) Reservation. Unfortunately, the *Seminole Indian News* was discontinued after only four issues, as Betty Mae became ill, and her recovery took much time.

Prince Albert of Monaco landed at the Big Cypress Aviation airfield during a visit to the Seminole Tribe of Florida. The tribe maintains the airfield, two helicopters, a fixed-wing airplane, and a corporate jet for the use of tribal members and visiting dignitaries. The plane and helicopters are also used for forestry work on the reservations.

Cattle and horses have played an important part in Seminole history, so perhaps it is not surprising that the Seminole Tribe of Florida operates the Big Cypress Rodeo Complex. Here tribe members and others participate in barrel racing and other rodeo events. Tribe members can also board horses at this facility.

As soon as she was able, she continued her other activities, and in 1967, at the age of forty-four, Betty Mae Tiger Jumper became the first elected chairman of the Seminole Tribe of Florida. In those days this was not a paid position, so she had to continue doing her regular job (coordinating the medical clinics on three reservations) while conducting important business for the tribe.

There was just 35 dollars in the tribal treasury when Betty Mae took office. By leasing reservation land, planting a lemon grove, and borrowing money from the federal government, she was able to increase the treasury to a half million dollars. She was also active in an organization called the United Southeastern Tribes, which united the Seminole and Miccosukee Tribes with the Mississippi Band of Choctaws and the Eastern Band of Cherokees for the purpose of **lobbying** Congress for needed services.

In 1970, President Richard Nixon appointed her to serve on the National Council on Indian Opportunity. That same year the National Seminar for

American Women named her one of the Top Indian Women of the Year. After her chairmanship was over, Betty Mae continued to be a spokeswoman for her tribe, and in 1984, she became the director of the Seminole Communications Department and editor in chief of the *Seminole Tribune*, then a biweekly newspaper. In 1994, she received the Folklife Heritage Award from the Florida Department of State, and Florida State University awarded her an honorary Doctor of Humane Letters degree. She was inducted into the Florida Women's Hall of Fame in 1995, and in 1997, the Native American Journalists Association awarded her its first Lifetime Achievement Award.

Former Oklahoma State Senator Enoch Kelly Haney has also made many contributions to the world. This talented Seminole/Creek artist and ***articulate*** statesman credits education and a supportive family with his success. He is a graduate of Bacone College and Oklahoma City University, from which he received a bachelor's degree in fine arts with a minor in religion. Enoch Kelly Haney was the first full-blooded Native American to win election to the Oklahoma State Legislature, where he served for six years before being elected to the Oklahoma State Senate. He served as a senator from 1986 through 2002. While a member of the Senate, he was a major force in drafting legislation regarding educational programs for at-risk students. He also took a leading role in the development of a Native American Cultural Center in Oklahoma City. In the 1970s, he was the host and producer of a television program that covered Native American issues on a weekly basis. He was also the narrator of series titled *How the West Was Lost*, which aired on the Discovery Channel. In addition to his work in television and politics, he has been a vocational counselor, served as a member of the ***adjunct faculty*** of Oklahoma City University, and been a member of the Oklahoma National Guard, as well as a planner/business manager for the Seminole Nation. On behalf of the United Methodist Church, he has served as a pastor and Regional Conference Youth Services Director. Enoch Kelly Haney is the recipient of more than eighty awards for community service and legislative leadership and has received international recognition for his paintings and sculptures.

In addition to the many accomplishments of individual Seminole, the Seminole Tribe of Florida has made a great contribution to the world through the preservation of tribal history at the Ah-tah-thi-ki Museum (located on the Big Cypress Reservation) and Okalee Indian Village and Museum (located on the Hollywood Reservation). Now families can travel

The Seminole Tribe of Florida operates a commercial citrus grove where juice oranges are grown.

back in time as they view authentic Seminole dress and other artifacts and learn about the culture of the Seminole people from the people themselves.

Anyone who desires to experience the Florida Everglades can do so thanks to Billie Swamp Safari, a 2,000-acre (809-hectare) **ecotourism** attraction located on the Big Cypress Reservation. There, visitors can take an airboat ride on the "river of grass" or jump on a "swamp buggy" for a land-based tour. People can see alligators and other native species, have lunch at the Swamp Water Café, and even spend the night in a chikee. We owe the Seminole our gratitude for the preservation of both South Florida history and environment and for sharing it with us in these ways.

The Florida Seminole are concerned about environmental issues. They want to preserve the untouched beauty of their land.

Chapter 8

Challenges for Today, Hopes for Tomorrow

Diabetes is a serious health concern for the Seminole in Oklahoma, since between 25 and 33 percent of tribal members are afflicted with this potentially life-threatening disease. The Seminole's new dialysis facility can service thirteen people at the same time, and it can accommodate four of these groups each day. The Seminole Nation is the first tribe in Oklahoma to have this type of facility.

Jamie Roden is in charge of Blackhills Dialysis, the new dialysis center of the Seminole Nation of Oklahoma. He explains that his clients need treatment three times per week, and they each spend an average of four hours on a machine. Most people pass the time by watching television, reading, knitting, or doing some other *sedentary* activity during dialysis. After treatment, they may be *lethargic*, and they can be somewhat confused. They also may suffer from cramps, and it can take a day to recover.

The dialysis center also offers wound care programs, because people with diabetes sometimes have wounds that do not heal easily. The facility has plans to hire a massage therapist, and they want to purchase exercise equipment. Additionally, the center houses a seminar room for educational use.

North American Indians did not usually suffer from this disease in the past, but it has become a growing concern, usually because of changes in diet and lack of exercise. Therefore, educational programs are an important means of tackling the disease.

Water quality and availability are another concern of the Florida Seminole today. Unlike diabetes, however, this issue had its beginnings more than a century ago when European settlers began to consider draining the Florida Everglades. The white settlers wanted more land for farming and buildings, and the first drainage canals were built in 1880. By the early 1900s, systematic drainage, coupled with a severe drought in 1913, had serious consequences for the Florida Seminole. Water gave them a means of traveling easily by canoe; drainage took that away from them. It also affected the wildlife upon which the Seminole were dependent for trade and hunting.

If you visit the Big Cypress Reservation today, you might notice heavy equipment and canals being dug along Alligator Alley (the road that leads from the highway to the reservation). This is a project aimed at shifting water that had been diverted to Miami back into the Everglades. The U.S. Army Corps of Engineers and the Seminole Tribe of Florida are sharing the cost of this project.

Water quality is also a concern of the tribe, since the natural flow of water from the north carries with it any heavy metals or impurities that it collects along the way. The U.S. Environmental Protection Agency (EPA) and the Seminole people are working together to comply with federal regulations to ensure proper water quality. The Seminole Tribe of Florida has maintained a Water Resource Management (WRMD) Department since 1987. The department evaluates both water and land resources and protects them by ensuring their wise use.

Using its right to tribal sovereignty, the Seminole Tribe of Florida developed a Tribal Water Code that established a legal means of restoration and protection of water on the reservations. The EPA granted the tribe the authority to implement the federal Clean Water Act.

The WRMD has many duties, including the sampling and analysis of water, as well as managing the data that is collected and the filing of reports with proper regional and federal agencies. The department also

Diabetes and Dialysis

People with diabetes cannot process sugar properly in their bodies. There are various ways of treating diabetes, including changes in diet, but sometimes the condition becomes so severe that the person needs dialysis. While a person receives dialysis, an artificial kidney works to purify the individual's blood.

Patients must be weighed before and after dialysis to make sure that the correct amount of fluid is being removed. The average person loses between eight and ten kilograms during a treatment.

works to prevent pollution in many ways; for example, it educates tribal members about the proper disposal of harmful products, and it gives tips on how to reduce their use. To help minimize the possibility of pollution, it also conducts scheduled pickups of used motor oil and industrial and household waste. The WRMD designs emergency response and spill con-

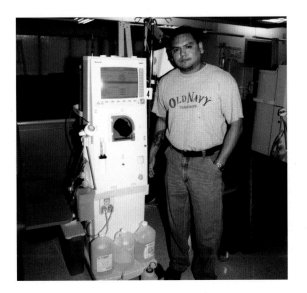

Jamie Roden stands beside a dialysis machine at Blackhills Dialysis in Oklahoma.

The Florida Seminole want to preserve the quality of water areas like this.
Drainage affects both their lifestyle and the wildlife that lives here.

trol plans to prevent or reduce pollution. It also provides assistance to
tribal members to be certain that any projects they are planning will not
adversely affect water quality.

The Seminole believe that "if the land dies, so will the tribe." That is one
of the reasons why they are actively involved in the restoration of the
ecosystem in South Florida. The Seminole Everglades Restoration Initiative
is a $65 million, multi-year project designed to increase water storage ca-
pacity, improve water quality, and enhance the water cycle.

In addition to health and environment matters, both the Seminole Tribe
of Florida and the Seminole Nation of Oklahoma are concerned about retaining their tribal languages. As the elders die, tribal languages are becoming endangered. Neither the Miccosukee language, which is spoken by
some members of the Seminole Tribe of Florida, nor Muscogee language,
which is spoken by other members of the tribe in Florida and by members
of the Seminole Nation of Oklahoma, was traditionally written. Although
there are some similar words in both languages, other words are completely different, so developing a united approach to preserving the languages would be difficult.

The Seminole Tribe of Florida has established a committee to save the languages and implemented a *language immersion* program. Preschools are now conducted exclusively in the tribal languages. As an incentive to get more speakers into homes with the children, the tribe pays parents to take language instruction one hour each day for five days a week.

According to Beverly Streater, Higher Education and Adult Education Director for the Seminole Nation of Oklahoma, a program was tried in some of the public schools in Oklahoma to introduce the Muscogee language, but it has been stalled. There are, however, efforts being made to reinstate Indian language programs and to introduce more Indian culture into Oklahoma public schools. She reports that the Seminole Nation was able to publish a language book and a second book is about to go to the printer. The Seminole Nation of Oklahoma has also received a library **grant** to conduct a summer program regarding the Seminole language.

Many of the goals of the Seminole Tribe of Florida and the Seminole Nation of Oklahoma are the same: improving the health of tribe members, im-

Casinos bring needed revenue to the reservations.

"If the land dies, so will the tribe." The Seminole are actively working to restore the Florida ecosystem.

proving and protecting the environment, creating educational and employment opportunities, and retaining tribal languages. Each group is strong willed, independent, and determined. Together, their people can achieve great things.

Sho-na-bish!
("Thanks!" in the Miccosukee language.)

Further Reading

Downs, Dorothy. *Art of the Florida Seminole and Miccosukee Indians.* Gainesville: University Press of Florida, 1995.

Jumper, Betty Mae Tiger and Patsy West. *A Seminole Legend: The Life of Betty Mae Tiger Jumper.* Gainesville: University Press of Florida, 2001.

Katz, William Loren. *Black Indians.* New York: Atheneum, 1986.

Lourie, Peter. *Everglades: Buffalo Tiger and the River of Grass.* Honesdale, Penn.: Boyds Mills Press, 1998.

Schultz, Jack M. *The Seminole Baptist Churches of Oklahoma.* Norman: University of Oklahoma Press, 1999.

Tiger, Buffalo and Harry A. Kersey Jr. *Buffalo Tiger: A Life in the Everglades.* Lincoln: University of Nebraska Press, 2002.

West, Patsy. *The Enduring Seminole: From Alligator Wrestling to Ecotourism.* Gainesville: University Press of Florida, 1998.

For More Information

The African-Native American History and Genealogy Webpage
www.African-Nativeamerican.com

Miccosukee Tribe of Indians of Florida
www.miccosukee.com/tribe.html

The Official Homepage of The Seminole Nation of Oklahoma
www.cowboy.net/native/seminole

The Seminole Tribe of Florida
www.seminoletribe.com

Tampa Bay History Center
www.tampabayhistorycenter.org/Seminole

Publisher's Note:

The Web sites listed on this page were active at the time of publication. The publisher is not responsible for Web sites that have changed their address or discontinued operation since the date of publication. The publisher will review and update the Web sites upon each reprint.

Glossary

acclimated: Adapted, becoming used to something.

adjunct faculty: Additional teachers that are called on occasionally and who work in addition to the regular staff.

adversely: To affect negatively.

airboat: A boat that is powered by a very loud motor with parts extending above the water.

animosity: Resentment.

annuities: Monetary payments made on a scheduled basis.

appliqué: The sewing of one piece of cloth (usually cut in a decorative shape) upon another.

arbor: A latticework covered with vines or leaves.

aromatic: Fragrant.

articulate: Well-spoken, effective, and clearly understood.

assimilation: To make people similar so they can fit into another culture.

bandolier: A belt that crosses the shoulder and supports something, such as a bag.

Bureau of Indian Affairs: The government agency that acts as an advocate for Indian needs.

cavalier: Offhand dismissal of important matters.

census: An attempt to locate and count a group of people.

chickee: A traditional Seminole house made of a palm thatch roof supported by cypress poles.

clan: An extended family group.

coercion: Trying to cause an action by threat or force.

configurations: The arrangement of the parts (buildings).

converted: Became a member of a religion different from the one previously practiced.

credo: A set of beliefs.

deception: Tricks and lies.

decimated: Destroyed.

denominations: Religious churches or organizations, each with its own specific set of beliefs.

dialysis: A medical treatment used when kidneys fail in which toxins are removed from the blood.

dispersed: Widely spread out or scattered.

duress: Threat and force.

early intervention: To provide assistance before a situation or condition develops or worsens.

ecosystem: The system of organisms and environment that function as a community.

ecotourism: Tourism that is based on allowing individuals to experience the natural environment without harming it.

elders: Older people who possess wisdom gained from age.

embroidery: Decorative stitching.

emerged: Came into view.

emetic: Something that is swallowed to induce vomiting.

emigrate: To leave one place in order to begin living in another.

empathy: To understand and identify with another person's feelings.

Everglades: A swampy area that covers the interior of southern Florida, sometimes called the "river of grass."

executive: Having the ability to administer and manage.

exhibition villages: Camps that were operated as tourist attractions in an effort to raise needed money for living.

faction: Group or part of a group.

GED: General Educational Development. A series of tests that, when passed, gives someone a high school equivalency certificate.

grant: Something, usually money, given for a particular purpose. Grants do not have to be repaid.

Head Start: A government program of preschool education for children from families meeting financial guidelines.

imminent: Going to happen very soon.

Indian agent: An official representative of the federal government to an American Indian tribe.

indigenous: Born to or occurring naturally in a particular region.

jitterbug: A popular dance during the 1930s.

judicial: The function of judging and moving through the court system.

language immersion: A teaching method in which only the language being learned is used.

legislative: The ability to make laws.

lethargic: Sluggish and slow moving.

lobbying: Influencing opinion through pressure or persuasion.

matriarchial: A situation in which descent and inheritance is traced through the mother.

medicine bundle: A group of sacred objects that are important to the well-being of the tribe and that are kept safe by a medicine man.

medicine men: Priestly healers.

nomadic: Roaming from place to place.

on commission: A term used when an artist has been hired to make a specific piece of art.

oral history: Stories that are passed from one person and one generation to another by being told, not written.

outbuildings: Buildings that are separate from and accessories to a main building.

palmetto: A type of palm.

perimeter: The edge or border around something.

periscopes: Optical instruments used to gain a view that cannot otherwise be seen, often used by submarines to see above the water.

persevered: Persisted, kept trying, didn't give up.

powwows: Social gatherings and celebrations of culture, often of many tribes, where arts and crafts are exhibited and sold and traditional dances can be observed.

proximity: Near to something.

purification: The act of making something clean.

reconciled: Settled, brought to just conclusion.

rendition: Version, interpretation.

renowned: Famous, highly acclaimed.

reservation: Land set aside for use by an American Indian tribe.

rituals: Established ceremonies.

sedentary: Without much movement, sitting.

segregation: Separating people from each other on the basis of a particular characteristic, often race.

smallpox: A highly contagious disease characterized by skin eruptions and scarring.

sovereign: Independent, possessing its own authority, autonomy, and absolute power.

sporadic: Occasional and not at specific intervals.

stomp dancing: Traditional Indian dancing that usually involves methodical movement, often in single file, around a fire.

tolerance: The capacity to allow something, such as a belief, that differs from your own.

traditionalists: People who believe in and continue to practice older, established customs.

transient: Moving from place to place.

tuberculosis: A highly contagious lung disease.

Index

Biographies

Joyce Libal is a writer and artist living with her husband and assorted pets on their orchard in the mountains of northeastern Pennsylvania. When she is not writing, Joyce enjoys painting, quilting, and gardening.

Martha McCollough received her bachelor's and master's degrees in anthropology at the University of Alaska-Fairbanks, and she now teaches at the University of Nebraska. Her areas of study are contemporary Native American issues, ethnohistory, and the political and economic issues that surround encounters between North American Indians and Euroamericans.

Benjamin Stewart, a graduate of Alfred University, is a freelance photographer and graphic artist. He traveled across North America to take the photographs included in this series.